I0492571

ITIL Foundation

Cheat Sheet

Muhammad Zeeshan Ali, PMP, PMI-ACP

Saqib Javed John, PMP, PMI-ACP, ITIL

Publications
2020

All inquiries should be addressed to (e-mail): publications@ogmcs.com

First Printing: 2020

ISBN: 9798713974398

OGMC Publications
publications.ogmcs.com

Ordering Information:
Special discounts are available on quantity purchases by corporations, associations, educators, and others. For details, contact the publisher at the above listed address.

Authors' Profile

Muhammad Zeeshan Ali

PMP, PMI-ACP

Saqib Javed John

PMP, PMI-ACP, ITIL

Author of multiple books and numerous articles elaborating new dimensions of Agile framework and Traditional Project Management along with his work on Performance Management, PMO, Leadership, Team Building and Personal Motivation. He is best known for designing first of its kind "Performance Measurement Matrix" to calculate number-based performance indicators and scoring for both Software Engineering Individuals and Teams. Zeeshan is a great advocate and promoter of adaptation of Agile Methodologies, Processes and Team Skill building.

Zeeshan has over 18 years of experience of managing 100+ mid-large scale, high visibility projects in both Public and Private sectors. Experienced in managing several significant projects simultaneously and with team spread over different geo-locations.

Zeeshan has Degrees in Project Management (MS) and Computer Sciences (BS). He has been certified as a Project Management Professional (PMP) and Agile Certified Professional (PMI-ACP) by Project Management Institute (PMI), USA.

Saqib is one of the founding members and Managing Director of Organizational Governance Management Consultants (OGMC). He has professional expertise of more than 18 years of working on enterprise projects in various business domains ranging from functional organization to projectized organization.

Saqib has immense experience in developing and managing human behavior, process engineering and optimization, risk management, conflict management, performance maturity audits and policy making. This is one of the reasons he is relatable to readers of Business and management professions. He is the best known for his rapid-learning techniques and easy methods of practical implementations. He also has contributed to many anthologies. His work is helping thousands of students, teachers and professionals.

Saqib is MS (IT), certified "Project Management Professional" (PMP) and "Agile Certified Practitioner" (ACP) from Project Management Institute (PMI) USA. He is also certified in "Information Technology Infrastructure Library" (ITIL) from Exin UK, "Sun Certified Java Programmer" (SCJP) and "Sun Certified Web Component Developer" (SCWCD) from Sun Microsystems USA.

Contents

1.0 Key Points for ITIL Exam

1.1 Key Points

1. Benefit of using ITIL is that the quality and the costs of the IT services can be controlled more efficiently

2. ITIL is so successful because It is not tied to any particular vendor platform

3. Incident: disruption to agreed service or a reduction in the quality of service

4. Problem: Unknown root cause of one or more incidents

5. Work-Around: Method of avoiding an incident or problem

6. "Event" is an occurrence that is significant for the management of the IT infrastructure or delivery of services

7. Customer perceptions and business outcomes help to define the "value of a service"

8. Service: Delivering value to customer without requiring the customer to own costs and risk

9. Trigger; event that launches a Process like call to service desk begins Incident Management activities

10. Common Sense approach "Do What Works"

11. A Known Error is raised after diagnosis of a Problem get completed

12. Request of changes (RFCs) resulting from Known Errors

13. Primary task of Error Control is to resolve Known Errors through the Change Management process

14. A Known Error database would be most useful in helping to implement a workaround as quickly as possible

15. To approve all modifications made to the Known Error database is the responsibility of Problem Management

16. Problem Management support the Service Desk activities by providing information on Known Error(s)

17. Service Strategy is about the selection of services; a service provider will offer to customer

18. Service strategy is the subset of Service portfolio

19. Service Strategy is MOST concerned with defining policies and objectives

20. All Processes of ITIL creates value for stakeholders

21. A process is continuous and has no end date, whereas a project has a finite lifespan.

22. "structuring an organization" is not a characteristic of Process

23. Every process will have Roles, Inputs & Outputs and Metrics

24. Activities, Guidelines and Standards may be defined in a Process

25. Processes: are the structured set of activities designed to achieve some specific objectives

    - Process Enablers: Resources and Capabilities; also known as input to process
    - A process responds to specific events
    - A process is performance driven and able to be measured

26. Good Practices: are best practices and may come from a number of sources including

    a. Standards
    b. Public Frameworks (ITIL, CMMI, Six Sigma
    c. Academic Research
    d. Proprietary Knowledge

27. Good Practice Is something that is in wide industry use

28. Outside of the core publications, The ITIL Complementary Guidance provides guidance in adapting good practice for specific business environments

29. ITIL core is structured around a service lifecycle

30. A Process owner is responsible for Monitoring and improving the Process

31. Change Management Process Owner is responsible for defining KPIs for Change Management

32. Process Owner is responsible for defining KPIs, Documenting the Process and Improving the Process

33. Only one - the process owner should be accountable for a process as defined in the RACI model

34. Service Owner, Process Owner & CSI Manager all are responsible of identifying opportunities for improvement

35. Process managers accountable for the operational management of a process

36. A Service Owner is responsible for Continual Improvement of the service

37. Service Owner: the person who is accountable for the delivery of specific service

38. More than one person can be responsible for activity but only one person can be accountable for activity

39. Resources and Capabilities are used to create value In form of services and goods

40. Knowledge Management; right information to right people at right time

41. Hierarchy used in knowledge management is Data - Information - Knowledge - Wisdom

42. The Configuration Management System is part of the Service Knowledge Management system

43. The KEDB (Known Error DB) and the CMS (Configuration Management System) form part of the larger SKMS (Service Knowledge Management System)

44. Backup of application data would not be stored in DML (Definitive Media Library)

45. The DML and Definitive Spares are the responsibility of Service Asset and Configuration Management

46. A DHS is an area set aside for the secure storage of definitive hardware spares

47. Definitive Media Library (DML) contains

48. The authorized and master copies of all software used on the infrastructure, Software licenses and controlled documentation are stored and protected in the Definitive Media Library (DML)

49. First activity of Continual Service Improvement is to understand the vision and high-level requirements of the business

50. Three main types of metrics of CSI Process; Process Metrics, Service Metrics and Technology Metrics

51. Components do Technology metrics measure

52. CSI provides guidance on improvement and measurement of processes and services

53. Learning and improvement is the primary concern of Continual Service Improvement

54. Activities aiming to improving an IT service are documented in Service Improvement Program (SIP)

55. "Service Improvement Program" is where activities documented with the aim of improving an IT service

56. Service metrics measure end to end service

57. "Functions" would NOT be defined as part of every process

58. Functions and Processes are also known as "specialized organizational capabilities"

59. Functions are self-contained units of an organization with their own capabilities and resources and provides structure and stability to organization

60. Functions rely on Process for cross-functional coordination and control

61. Functions are also known as departments like service desk, Operations and Application management

62. Function "IT Operations Management" is responsible for monitoring activities and events in IT Infrastructure

63. IT Operations Management includes IT Operations Control and Facilities Management

64. Operations Control refers to the overseeing the execution and monitoring of IT operational events & activities

65. Event Management is responsible for monitoring an IT Service and detecting when the performance drops below acceptable limits

66. Facilities Management refers to the management of the Physical IT Environment such as a data center

67. Application management is not responsible for developing functionality required by the business
68. "First point of customer contact" is a Service Desk
69. key attributes needed by Service Desk Staff are business awareness, articulate; methodical, tolerant and good interpersonal skills
70. "Number of hardware faults reported" is not valid performance indicators for the Service Desk
71. "Solving a Problem" or "Diagnosing root-cause of Problem" is not the activity of Service Desk
72. Service Desk is responsible for tracking and monitoring an incident
73. Request fulfillment and Incident management are performed by the service desk
74. Following should be available to the Service Desk
    a. Known Error Data
    b. Change Schedules
    c. Service Knowledge Management System
    d. Diagnostic scripts and tools
75. Centralized service desk; There is a single desk in one location serving the whole organization
76. The purpose of Request Fulfillment Process is dealing with Service Requests from the users
77. Objective of request fulfillment; to provide info to users what services are available and how to request them
78. Request Fulfillment process is responsible for low risk, frequently occurring, low cost changes

79. Request to change the functionality of an application is not Service Request

80. The main reason of establishing a Baseline is for later comparisons

81. Configuration Baseline is a recorded snapshot of a product or service, to provide a basis for a configuration audit and regression

82. Baseline in the IT infrastructure is a standard configuration

83. Availability Management is responsible for availability of Components, Services and Resources

84. In Availability Management, CIA terms stand for Confidentiality, Integrity and Availability

85. Like IT Service Continuity Management, Availability Management is another processes that could also initiate precautionary measure

86. Availability Management ensures that service availability matches or exceeds the agreed needs of the business

87. Availability Management process uses Mean Time Between Failures (MTBF)

88. Availability Management work with Security Management by implementing the measures specified by Security Management for securing the data

89. Reliability is that how long a service or component can perform its function without failing

90. Serviceability; The degree of support that the Service Desk provides to the customer

91. The concept of "Post Implementation Review" is part of Change Management

92. "Remediation Planning" is the stage of the Change Management process deals with what should be done if the change is unsuccessful

93. Change Management process is responsible for the replacement of any IT equipment

94. A change to a business process would fall outside the scope of a typical service change management process

95. If Change Management is implemented without Configuration Management; the result will be less effective

96. "Ongoing or concluded Changes" should be one of the standard items on the agenda of a meeting of the Change Advisory Board (CAB)

97. In case of complex change, The Change Manager presents the change to the Change Advisory Board

98. Remediation Planning is planning the steps required to be taken if a change is unsuccessful

99. The planning of changes kept up to date in the FSC (Forward Schedule of Changes)

100. Configuration Management is responsible for registering modification in the Configuration Management DB and can only be modified after permission is granted to modify the infrastructure by Change Management

101. Configuration Management help to monitor the IT services

102. Configuration Management provides Details and history of the IT infrastructure

103. Statuses of changes recorded in the Configuration Management Database (CMDB)

104. Asset Management monitors aspects such as depreciation and Configuration Management monitors aspects such as the relationships between the Configuration Items.

105. Configuration Management System (CMS) can help to determine the level of impact of a problem

106. Recording the relations between Configuration Items is the responsibility of Configuration Management

107. A call, A user name, An incident or A process is not the Configuration Item (CI)

108. Hardware, Documentation, Staff, Software, Network components all are Configuration Items

109. Configuration Management goes much further than Asset Management, because it also specifies the relations between the assets.

110. The Application Portfolio contains key attributes of all applications, The Application Portfolio is sometimes implemented as part of the Service Portfolio, or as part of the Configuration Management System

111. The objective of Asset and Configuration Management is To define and control the components of services and infrastructure and maintain accurate configuration records

112. "IT Service Continuity Management" provides assurances for the provision of IT services in case of an interruption in the services

113. "IT Service Continuity Management" aims to trace business-critical services for which supplementary emergency measures must be taken

114. Risk analysis carries out in IT Service Continuity Management

115. Access Management is responsible for

    a. Verifying the identity of users requesting access to services

    b. Setting the rights or privileges of systems to allow access to authorized users

    c. Is sometimes referred to as Rights Management or Identity Management.

116. Confidentiality ensures that data must only be accessible by authorized users

117. Access Management is closely related to Information Security Management

118. Its "Business" who provides the primary guidance on what protection Information Security Management should provide for each asset

119. The Information Security Policy should be available to All customers, users and IT staff

120. The process of Incident Management is used to take queries of both internal and external incidents

121. In Incident Management Process level of working group sequences is, First line Service Desk, Second line Solutions Teams and Third Line Specialists

122. Incident Management has a value to the business by Contributing to the reduction of impact

123. an Incident Model, a set of pre-defined steps to be followed when dealing with a known type of Incident

124. An incident model contains Chronological order of steps to resolve the incident not the detailed SAL

125. Major Incidents require Separate procedures

126. Incidents can be reported by anyone who detects a disruption or potential disruption to normal service, This includes technical staff

127. An Incident which has a high priority or high impact on the business is known as Major Incident

128. All incidents must be fully logged

129. Service Level Management responsible to create a customer facing service catalogue

130. Supplier Management and Service Level Management processes regular review underpinning contracts

131. Operational Level Agreement (OLA) is an agreement between the service provider and another part of the same organization

132. Service Level Management process reviews Operational Level Agreements (OLAs) on a regular basis

133. An organization determines the effectiveness of the Service Level Management Process by measuring customer satisfaction

134. "Service Level Management" use data from the Service Desk's incident registration to analyze, together with other data, in order to determine if the agreed service level is being provided

135. Service Level Requirements are used in the Service Level Management process represent the customer's expectations and needs regarding the service

136. If something cannot be measured, then it should not be documented in Service Level Agreement

137. Full Service Level Agreements is NOT the part of IT Service Continuity Plan

138. In relation to IT Service Continuity Planning, the severity of a disaster depends upon the impact upon customers' businesses

139. Agreements regarding Security Management recorded in a Service Level Agreement (SLA)

140. A Service-based Service Level Agreement(SLA) covers one service, for all the customers of that service

141. Multi-level Service Level Agreement (SLA) covers Corporate, Customer, Service

142. A Service Level Agreement(SLA) is the place where incident resolution targets to be documented

143. SLA Monitoring Chart (SLAM) is a document to see an overview of actual service achievements against targets

144. The quality of the services offered are described in SLA

145. Budgeting and accounting are the two mandatory elements of Financial Management

146. Reviewing IT service quality is NOT the concern of IT Financial Management

147. The concept of "Procuring" is not the part of Financial Management for IT Services

148. Problem: The unknown cause of one or more incidents

149. Incident Records is the input to the Problem Management process

150. Problem Management is responsible for tracing the cause of an error

151. An objective of Problem Management is to restore normal service operation as quickly as possible and minimizing adverse impact on the business

152. Implementation of the Problem Management process can cut down the percentage of regularly recurring incidents

153. "Error Control" is the activity in the Problem Management process which is responsible for generating Requests for RFCs

154. "Categorization" is the problem management's activity ensures that a problem can be easily tracked and management information can be obtained

155. Problem management is responsible for eliminating recurring incidents and minimizing the impact of incidents that cannot be prevented

156. Service Management is a set of specialized capabilities for delivering value to customers in form of services.

157. IT Service Management contribute to the Quality of IT service provision by Planning, Implementing and Managing a coherent set of processes for providing IT services

158. The role of ITIL within IT Service Management is to provide an approach based on the best examples taken from practice

159. "Interrelated Activities" is the basis of the ITIL approach to Service Management

160. The Plan-Do-Check-Act cycle can be used to plan and implement Service Management Processes, each stage should be carried out once in the order Plan-Do-Check-Act

161. Performance Management and Resource Management are parts of Capacity Management process

162. Performance information that supports the Capacity Management process be stored in capacity management information system (CMIS)

163. Capacity Management that makes the most use of data supplied by Demand Management

164. Demand Management is primarily used to Eliminate excess capacity needs

165. Differential charging is a technique used in Demand Management

166. Patterns of demand are driven by patterns of business activity

167. Capacity Management process contains the Business, Service and Component sub-processes

168. Capacity Managements responsible for ensuring the organization is aware of new and changing technology

169. Application Sizing is a technique used by Capacity Management that means "The resources needed for an application and its performance can be predicted"

170. Modeling activity belongs to Capacity Management

171. Countermeasures for risks is not the part of Capacity Plan

172. Service Operations should maintain a balance between an internal IT view and an external business view

173. Good communication is essential for successful Service Operation, just as for any other phase of the Lifecycle

174. The Service Portfolio has information about all services; the Service Catalogue only has information about services which are live and operational, or being prepared for deployment

175. RACI Model would be most useful in helping to define an organizational structure

176. The RACI model is beneficial to design Function

177. RACI model is used for documenting the roles and relationships of stakeholders in a process or activity

178. Release and Deployment Management process is
    a. To ensure there are clear release and deployment plans
    b. To ensure that skills and knowledge are transferred to operations and support staff
    c. To ensure there is minimal unpredicted impact on production services

179. Big bang vs. Phased, Push and Pull and Automated vs. Manual are the options discussed in Release and Deployment Management

180. Release Management process is responsible to store original versions of all authorized softwares

181. Release Management process is responsible for ensuring that updated version is tested

182. Release Management is responsible for the correct configuring and transmission of the programs

183. If release proved defective, Release Management will implement the back-out plan

184. "The risk register for the release" would NOT be contained in a release policy

185. The portion of a service or IT infrastructure that is normally released together is called Release Unit

186. A single Release unit, or a structured set of Release units can be defined within a Release Package

187. Compiling the release schedule is the first activity when implementing a release

188. Insourcing relies on internal resources; outsourcing relies on external organization(s) resources

189. Co-Sourcing is a Combination of Internal & External Sourcing

190. Knowledge Process Outsourcing (KPO) provides domain based business expertise

191. Supplier Management should be involved in all stages of the service lifecycle, from Strategy through Design and Transition to Operations and Improvement

192. Supplier Management don't negotiate internal and external agreements to support the delivery of services

193. Development, negotiation and agreement of contracts are the responsibilities of Supplier Management.

194. Supplier Management process is responsible for managing relationships with vendors but not for Managing relationships with internal suppliers

195. An objective of business relationship management is to ensure high levels of customer satisfaction

196. Normally four processes are involved in achieving a structural solution i.e. Incident, Change, Configuration, Release & Problem Management

197. A Service Provider (Organization) is one who supplying services to one or more internal or external customers

198. Internal, External and Shared Service Provider are the three Service Provider business models

199. The "Service Provider" owns the specific costs and risks associated with providing a service

200. Percentage availability is calculated as (Agreed Service Time – Downtime) x 100 / Agreed Service Time

201. Following a process or delivering an IT service, the result of carrying out an activity is known as "Outcome"

202. Designing and maintaining all necessary service transition packages is NOT part of the service design stage

203. A Service design package (SDP) would normally be produced for
    a. A new IT service
    b. A major change to an IT service
    c. An IT service retirement

204. A benefit of using Service Design tools is to help ensure that standards and conventions are followed

205. Service Trans Service strategies value to the business as enabling the service provider to have a clear understanding of what levels of service will make their customers successful

206. Without a good Accounting System, you cannot:
    a. Know the full cost of services provided
    b. Judge the efficiency of Problem Management
    c. Recover costs related to usage, should you so wish

207. Service Transition provides guidance on moving new and changed services into production, guidance for testing and

guidance for the transfer of services to or from an external service provider

208. Business drivers and requirements for a new service should be considered during review of the current capabilities of IT service delivery

209. Service V model represent

    a. A strategy for the successful completion of all Service Management projects

    b. The path to Service Delivery and Service Support for efficient and effective utilization of resources

210. Details of a workaround always be documented in "The Problem Record"

211. Objectives of Service Design

    a. To satisfy business objectives

    b. Identify and manage risk

    c. Design effective and efficient processes

    d. Design a secure and resilient IT infrastructure

212. "Governance" is concerned with fairness and transparency

213. Service Design is the stage where processes needed to operate a new service be defined

214. PRIMARY concern of the IT Governance is to ensure that processes and procedures are correctly followed

215. The underpinning contracts used to document the provision of goods and services by Suppliers

216. Request Models used for defining how frequently received user requests should be handled

217. Service Design is MOST concerned with the design of new or changed services

218. The consequences of the change such as limited, substantial, significant, etc. defines a category for a change

219. Mean Time to Repair (MTTR) means "Average downtime of a service"

220. Fault Tolerance; The ability of an IT Service or Configuration Item to continue to operate correctly after failure of a component part.

221. Proprietary Knowledge may be difficult to adopt, replicate or transfer since it is often undocumented

222. Within Service Design, the key output handed over to Service Transition is "Service Design Package"

223. Service Pipeline contains all services that are at a conceptual or development stage

224. Normally four processes are involved in achieving a structural solution i.e. Incident, Change, Configuration, Release & Problem Management

225. Open-Loop System Perform an activity regardless of environment conditions i.e. backup Schedule

226. Closed-Loop System Monitor environment and respond to changes i.e. load balancing

227. Business Case Structure
    a. Introduction
    b. Methods and Assumptions
    c. Business Impacts
    d. Risk and Contingencies
    e. Recommendation

228. Sequence of events in the selection of a technology tool Requirements, Selection Criteria, Evaluate Product, Select Product

2.0   Quick Exam Notes

2.1 Cheat Sheet

1. ITIL consist of PP-TC Processes, Procedures, Tasks and Checklists
2. ITIL Manage CK-RR Capabilities, Knowledge, Risk and Resources
3. Capabilities PP-KMO (People, Processes, Knowledge, Management, Organization)
4. Resources FCI-API (Financial, Capital, Infrastructure, Applications, People, Information)
5. ITIL Provides Services through CCDDN (Collaboration, Coordination, Direction, Delegation, Network)
6. History (initial draft 1980 by CCTA, V2 2001 by CCTA & OGC, V3 2007 by OGC, Revised V3 2011 by HM Government
7. Life Cycle Modules [ON, Implement] (SS, SD, ST, SO)
8. Capability Modules [IN, Execution] (SOA, PPO, RCV, OSA)
9. Service Strategy PDF (Portfolio, Demand, Financial]
10. Service Design ACCCSSS (Availability, Capacity, Continuity, Catalog, Supplier, Security, Service Level)
11. Service Transition CCR (Change, Configuration, Release)
12. Service Operations AE-ISP (Access, Event, Incident, Service Desk, Problem)
13. CSI Supporting Models and Processes (PDCA, CSI Model, CSI 7 Steps)
14. CSI Model (What is the vision, where are we Now, where do we want to be, how do we get there, did we get there, how do we maintain momentum)

15. CSI 7 Steps (Define what you should measure, define what you can measure, Gather the data, Process the data, Analyze the data, Present the data, Implement improvement or Corrective Actions)

16. Function is Service Operations AITS (Service Desk, Technical Management, Application Management and IT Ops Management)

17. Information Systems ACCCKKSS (Availability, Capacity, Catalog, Configuration, Knowledge, Known Error, Supplier and Security)

18. Roles (Service Manager, Product Manager, Service Owner, Process Owner)

19. 5 Core Processes of ISO 20K CD-RRR (Delivery, Control, Relationship, Resolution, Release)

20. Delivery Models ICOM-BK (In-sourcing, Co-sourcing, Multi-Sourcing, Out-sourcing, BPO, KPO)

21. V Model RAOTR (Review, Acceptance, Operational, Testing, Release)

22. Kano Model factors (Basic factors, Excitement factors, Performance factors)

23. 4 P's of Service Strategy (Perspective, Position, plan, pattern)

24. 4 P's of Service Design (People, Processes, Product, Partners)

25. Seven R's of Change Management (Raised, Reason, Return, Risk, Resources, Relationship, Responsible)

26. Types of Changes NSE (Normal, Standard, Emergency)

27. Seven Steps of Change Management RRE-API-R (Record, Review, Evaluate, Authorize, Plan, Implementation, Review & Close)

28. Types of Service Providers (Type 1[Internal], Type 2[Shared], Type 3[External])

29. Service Desk Configurations (Local, Virtual, Centralized, Follow-the-Sun)

30. Types of Events (Regular Operations, Warnings, Exceptions)

31. Types of Escalations (Vertical/Hierarchical, Horizontal/Functional)

32. Types of Measurements PC-DR-R (Preventive, Corrective, Detective, Reductive, Repressive)

33. Purposes of Measurements JDIV (To Justify, To Direct, To Intervene, To Valuate)

34. Value = Utility + Warranty

35. Warranty ACCS (Availability, Capacity, Continuity, Security)

36. Priority = Impact + Urgency

37. Aspects of Availability RMS (Reliability, Maintainability, Serviceability)

38. Capacity Management DRS-CT (Demand, Resource, Service, Component, Threshold)

39. Characteristics of Configuration Item (CI) CARS (Category, Attributes, Relationship, Status)

40. Costing Units ESOTA (Organization, Equipment, Transfer, Accommodation and Software)

41. Five aspects of Service Design TPS4M (Technology, Processes, Solution, Management, Measurement, Methods and Metrics)

42. Constraints of Design WU-RCCP (Warranty, Utility, Resources, Capabilities, Contractual, Pricing, Standards and Regulations, Values and Ethics, Copyright, Patent and Trademarks)

43. Portfolio Management methods DAAC (Define, Approve, Analyze, Charter)

44. Portfolio Service Groups (Pipeline, Catalog and Retired)

45. Five elements of Security Framework PIC-ME (Plan, implement, Control, Maintain, Evaluate)

46. Basic qualities of Information Asset CIA-AN (Confidentiality, Integrity, Availability, Authenticity, Non-Repudiation)

47. Balancing Portfolio Management (Run Business, Transform Business and Grow Business)

48. Information Security Policy covers (Password, Email, Virus Control, Encryption, Remote Access)

49. Seven steps for change management (Record, Review, Evaluate, Authorize, Plan, Implantations, Review and close)

50. Continual Service Improvement Metrics (cannot Define cannot Measure, cannot Measure cannot Control, cannot Control cannot Manage)

3.0   Important Exam Tips

3.1 Exam Tips

1. Usually people stop reading a day before exam but we must advise that please do not stop and keep revising the things as its very important to revise even those things which you know very well.

2. Don't invest time on such questions where you find very long descriptions or the questions giving you impression of difficulty and confusion. To manage such question, select any better option and put that question(s) on revision this way you can keep yourself away from going under the time pressure.

3. In order to give the right answer, you must be very sure about the three wrong answers, more or less this is the only way to give the confirmed right answer.

4. In Test/Exam room, you will get blank papers with couple of led pencils, use first 15 mins (i.e. Exam Tutorial Time) to write down the key points and formulas given in cheat sheet.

5. Must attempt the calculations based questions even if it takes little more time than the average because on such questions you will know there and then that your answer is right or wrong.

6. Keep concentrating on questions and don't eye much on the time clock, check your velocity only after 20 or 40 or 50 questions. It's a high speed exam, even seconds are important, analyzing the answering speed again and again will be time wasting and keep you under pressure.

7. Read well the question and all answers, before deciding the correct answer, if you are confused between 2 very close options

then read the question again at least two times because usually solution of that ambiguity is hidden in question.

8.   Try to reach at testing center one hour earlier than your exam time because testing center staff will also give you brief regarding exam rules etc. along with the few standard tips, listen to them even if you are already aware with rules/tips.

Other Books from OGMC Publications

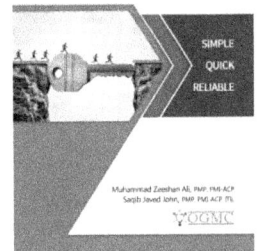

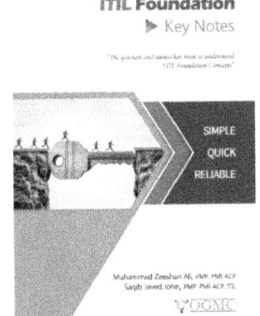

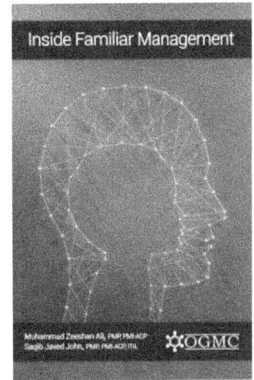

Publications
PUBLICATIONS.OGMC.COM

.